Golden Boy 1999

AUDREY WALKER

Flora 1999 (detail)

Foreword

When the history of British textile art – an emergent practice with its roots, variously, in the post war craft revival, in feminist debates of the 70s and 80s, in the particular histories of the textile crafts of weaving, dyeing, printing and embroidery, and in the broader history of the visual arts in the 20th century – comes to be written, the name of Audrey Walker will figure prominently. She will appear as a maker who has used a background in painting to push continually at the boundaries of stitched textiles in developing her own work. She will also be singled out for introducing, when Head of Department at Goldsmiths', the kind of inter-disciplinary thinking which is now so fashionable by extending the remit of the course from embroidery to the more synoptic textiles, and for encouraging her students to explore ideas first, and only then to seek out the history and techniques which they needed to realise them. It is precisely this kind of catholic thinking which makes textiles practice currently so vibrant and self-confident.

These are the 'parallel lives' described so eloquently by Amanda Fielding in this catalogue. For the first time, however, a national touring solo exhibition allows us to celebrate publicly the essentially more private of those lives. I wish Audrey and Ruthin Craft Centre every success with it.

Jennifer Harris
Deputy Director and Curator of Textiles
The Whitworth Art Gallery, Manchester

Flora 1999

Contents

Introduction

Audrey Walker's most recent work is a rich yet subtle exploration of the human gaze and encounter, revealing strength and presence in the emergent portraits. This interest in figurative imagery originated in her student days, struggling with the challenges, complexities and particular disciplines of portraiture. In her own words 'my most recent work has come full circle to a preoccupation I had when I was a student: working with ideas about heads, people glancing at each other, inward smiles'. She continues to be inspired by and to connect with archaic icons, expressive fragments of Greek sculpture, the stylised rendering of Coptic weave, the arch expressions or calm solidity of Piero della Francesca's subjects, or inscrutable tomb portraits from Roman Egypt.

The pieces here further explore that sense of connection between the ancient and contemporary, fixing the transient glance, rendering the immediate qualities of an encounter timeless, accentuating a nuance... She attains this in her portraits through careful analysis of her subjects, followed by a cycle of contemplation, sketching, stitching, revisiting – through gradual layering adding form, light and depth, the recognisable human irregularities and inward secrets to be deduced – perhaps if Virginia Woolf had stitched this is what it would be like.

Audrey Walker spent seven years training as a painter, firstly at Edinburgh College of Art, and then at the Slade School of Fine Art. She began making embroideries in the early 1960s, ten years after leaving art school, and taught embroidery in schools and colleges becoming Head of the Embroidery and Textile Department at Goldsmiths College from 1975 to 1988. Her embroideries are in public and private collections in the UK (including the V&A Museum), Australia, Canada, Eire, Italy and the USA, and have been profiled in many books and journals. She is now based in Pembrokeshire and was awarded an MBE for her services to textiles in 1993.

This is (incredibly) Audrey Walker's first solo exhibition. It profiles a new body of stitched-pieces and the development of the ideas involved through drawings. While she was developing ideas and producing pieces for the exhibition textile artist Dr Polly Binns visited her at her studio and in the essay 'Conversation on a Working Day' comments on her working process. In the essay 'Parallel Lives: Audrey Walker, Embroiderer and Teacher' Amanda Fielding, Curator of the Crafts Council Collection and an influential commentator on the applied arts, discusses the broader aspects of Audrey Walker's career.

During the process of researching a solo exhibition one inevitably talks to a great number of people about the artist and their work. With Audrey Walker both the numbers and the diversity of those

Fragment (i) 1999

Fragment (ii) 1999 (right)
Fragment (iv) 1999 (left)

who talked about her work was staggering. They ranged from Embroiders' Guild members who spoke with great warmth at being inspired by her work for more than thirty years; visitors to several textile exhibitions (those starting a conversation saying 'Life is just a bowl of cherries' before enthusing about that and several other pieces, too numerous to mention); to internationally renowned textile artists. This began when I visited Eleri Mills, to discuss plans for Eleri's solo exhibition in 1994, during the inevitable process of artist and curator finding out where each is 'coming from' the conversation turned to Audrey Walker – Eleri was unequivocal in her assessment of her importance and uniqueness. Thus six years on (it took a while to persuade Audrey to do this exhibition) we asked textile practitioners – Michael Brennand-Wood, Shelly Goldsmith, Rozanne Hawksley, Alice Kettle and Eleri Mills – to comment on why Audrey Walker has been such an important influence to so many. We are most grateful to all the above for their contributions, to the Arts Council of Wales for funding this exhibition, and to everyone else who has worked so hard to make it happen.

I am particularly grateful to Dr Jennifer Harris, Deputy Director and Curator of Textiles at the Whitworth Art Gallery in Manchester, author of several influential publications on Textiles including *Five Thousand Years of Textiles* and curator of several major exhibitions including *The Subversive Stitch* in 1988, for her invaluable help and advice with the production of this catalogue and for agreeing to formally open the exhibition at Ruthin.

Finally, I am sure that all of those who have enjoyed Audrey Walker's work over the years and newcomers visiting this exhibition to see her work for the first time will wish to thank her for her continued, and outstanding contribution to the canon of contemporary textiles.

The exhibition will open at The Gallery, Ruthin Craft Centre in May 2000 and then it will tour nationally throughout the UK.

Philip Hughes, Gallery Director, Ruthin Craft Centre

Fragment (iii) 1999

Encounters and endeavours

The drawings and embroideries which I have brought together for this exhibition have been produced, with only a few exceptions, since early summer 1999. This is just a short period in a longish working life but it reflects my abiding interest in figurative imagery.

It would be ridiculous to deny the huge importance and influence of abstraction in 20th Century art but I have always admired it at a distance and have found myself more intrigued and moved by work which engages with the human condition.

There is a continuity of figuration from pre-history carving to present day video, across cultures and in every possible medium. Textiles, as I continue to discover, have a rich seam to mine in this respect, and I feel I have barely scratched the surface of possibilities.

About the embroideries:

For several years I have been concentrating on heads drawn from memory. I am fascinated by momentary glances, encounters, inward smiles. I am enthralled by the way that even centuries-old images can still make powerful connections with us today. I try to make work which is suggestive rather than descriptive of these encounters leaving the viewer with some work to do. I have sometimes been challenged to say whether the image is male or female and, although I know what I began with, I am not troubled if there is some ambiguity in the end. What matters is whether the gaze is strong enough.

The materials and methods are relatively simple. A variety of fabrics is laid down to establish broad areas of tone and colour. Layer upon layer of simple stitching is then built up to develop the image. This may be done by hand or machine stitching depending upon the mark that is needed. Occasionally a defining or correcting mark is made with acrylic paint. Sometimes worked areas are cut out, re-positioned or replaced. The final image is only partly sensed at the beginning and emerges through the making.

About the drawings:

Stitching is a slow process and rapid gestures are just about unattainable with needle and thread. Cutting, piecing, wrapping and collaging are of course possible. However, for most of the time I am layering a surface slowly, mark by individual mark. Probably, for this reason, I thoroughly enjoy the time I take away from my workroom to share an afternoon's drawing with a group of friends and a model. A few drawn lines can allow for discoveries which may be absorbed into memory. Graphite, charcoal and chalk are immediately effective media.

Temptation 1999

Study – Temptation 1999
Smiling couple 1999 (left)

Drawn portraits are attempts to describe particular characteristics of friends. I try to remain fairly detached when I'm making these drawings, hoping to allow a sensation beyond the outward appearance to emerge. This 'sensation beyond appearance' makes the link in my mind with my other work, particularly the embroideries – my concern with the connection between viewer and image – an encounter, a gaze, and the sitter's own pre-occupations.

Other drawings, from memory and imagination, are more closely related to the embroideries. They are made alongside, before or after the stitching and are not intended as 'designs', but as thoughts around the same subject. Quite often they are made at the end of a day's stitching, almost as a critique of that day's work. At other times they simply express an idea which needs to be held for future reflection. They exist in their own right.

About labels:

I like the description 'maker'. It is wonderfully direct and applies whether we make paintings or poems, films, sculpture, ceramics, jewellery, textiles…

Craftsmanship is essential for eloquence in any medium and many of the tediously worn out arguments about 'fine art' or 'craft' might be set aside if it could be agreed that we are engaged in a common endeavour to make things with as much conviction – eloquence – as we can manage. We might then be able to look at all kinds of work without prejudice identifying its maker's aims and ambitions more sympathetically. We might locate 'function' in painting as well as in pots. We could attempt to understand metaphor (and thus 'art') regardless of the medium but with respect for, and interest in, diverse histories and traditions. Whether I stitch, draw or paint the thinking is the same.

Audrey Walker

Studies:

Night Window 1999 (right)

Woman at a Window (ii) 1999 (below left)

Woman at a Window (iii) 1999 (below right)

Woman at a Window (i) 1999 (left)

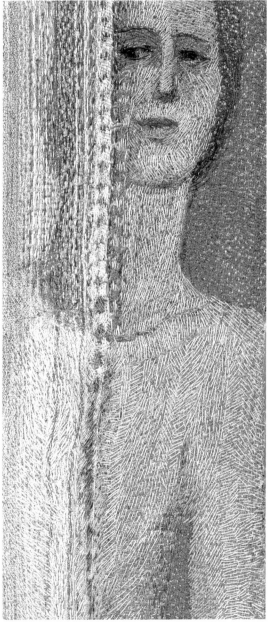

Woman at the window 1999
(above and detail left)

Who's There? 1999 (right)

Conversation on a working day

What is written here is based on an extended conversation I enjoyed with Audrey Walker in her studio, several months prior to the opening of this exhibition. We explored that most vulnerable of subjects, the mysterious way in which the artist negotiates their creative preoccupation and the sense of the convoluted journey within and between works which accumulate into an exhibition.

Our common ground was a shared acknowledgement of the reluctance to express in words, fragile and intangible aspects of the creative process. Therefore, the frankness and patience with which Audrey Walker did discuss her work was both illuminating and deeply rewarding.

In her preoccupation with stitch lie clear memories of her training as a painter. She thinks and feels and acts in the same way whether working with a brush and paint or with a needle and thread. In citing relationships to methods learnt in her original training, she does not validate her textile activity through that Fine Art experience, but rather sees them as separate but related activities exploring similar concerns. Painting plays an intrinsic role in the development of her work through layered washes of colour or the laying down of painted sections of gauze. Stitch has primacy. Both machine and hand stitching, used together, develop the surface, creating simple and variable straight marks.

The current work is rich in this multiplicity of stitch. Each mark is placed with that seemingly effortless sureness that is only achieved through the rigour of making where the process employed is the essential support to the development of ideas. This knowledge of her material is expressed through her determination not to be self consciously aware of making the stitch but to be uncontrived and intuitive. If she becomes aware of pattern and of seeing stitch before the mark and the medium then it won't 'do' for her.

In the studio she works with an immense palette of thread around her, arranged as her current needs require. She rejoices in her passion for colour referring to her thread as lines of pure colour, colour which as it is layered down cannot become blurred as with paint.

Each study is worked on fabric stretched over a frame, which allows the work to be moved around easily. She mostly sits to stitch but is always alert to the seductive intimacy of 'surface at arms length' and consciously moves pieces around the studio to allow her a middle distance view, in different light and at different heights. She frequently sets work up in the studio opposite to the glass entrance door, which allows her, as she approaches the studio, an objective distance viewing as if in a gallery.

The composition of each piece is a spontaneous and fluid development over the whole field of the

Eve 2000

the work, by re-layering sections onto a new background and building the composition anew. If two hours, or even two days, of concentrated stitch isn't 'doing' what she wants then it has to go. She is never 'precious' about the effort involved in the development of her work. Every element of the process employed must be 'essential' and 'true to her observation'.

For approximately the last six years, these observations have been with the figure and with a focus to the gaze. She acknowledges, looking back in retrospect, that she has always been drawn to exhibitions about the figure across the broadest cultural remit and especially towards images and objects which 'drew the viewer in' either as a direct recipient to the gaze from figures in the work, or to where the viewer bears witness to 'uneasy' relationships manifested through the gaze between figures within a composition. She is fascinated that the gaze both evokes and transcends reality, that an image can speak to us, connect unmediated with our own lives irrespective of the centuries or of the cultural understandings which lie between us.

Starting points for work are fleeting gestures, the half-won glimpse remembered. An essence of

work. Stitching an area is dependent on the sense of the colour and the tone next to it. There is no prescribed order of working; paint and stitch is layered and insinuated within the whole in response to the individual development understood for each work. Radical re-structuring and re-thinking can occur and is achieved by cutting into

Eve 2000 (work in progress)
Adam 2000 (right and detail above)

the work is the impermanence of the moment and the negotiation of how to synthesize that impermanence. For her a transitory moment made permanent has a life but in its tangibility must evoke impermanence. Also, imbued within the work is her own sense of the moment, of its fading away and the replacing of other senses of memory, throughout her working preoccupation. In the direction in which a work may develop she is receptive to layerings of memory within her creativity and to the seeming dichotomies which this sense can both span and encompass. The moment a work succeeds is an intangible experience, a factor of the moment when a work has a 'rightness, its own life'. The question the work asks may only become apparent once the answer is found.

Integral to the development of her observations is the activity of drawing. She refers to drawing as 'essential; very enjoyable'. One wall in the studio acts as an open sketchbook filled with 'drawn' thinking stages. Unlike a book-based sketchbook where a permanent page order implies a narrative, a sequential history to the creative process, the studio wall acts as a constantly changing and evolving negotiation of ideas. She discusses her drawing as both initiating an idea articulated in stitch and also to drawing as a confirming process, at the end of the working day, a way of acutely responding to the development of a stitched piece. The discipline of drawing enacts a synthesizing role, a layering of process and of engagement with her perceived observations within the creative journey.

There is, in the way she discusses her work, an overarching sense of layering in her negotiation of memory, the nuances of meaning within the work and also with the physicality of making. The demands she makes for the work are rigorous and complex. The point of exhibition is seen as an opportunity to stand back and reflect but to accept its transience. For her, to focus the work in the public gaze is part of the continuing evolution. In the same way, the articulation of her 'creative journey' for this catalogue essay should be read as

part of that evolution. It can offer no fixed meaning to the work, offer no definitive statement. A conversation on a working day only forms a particular layer in the accumulated oeuvre. The work has already moved beyond.

Polly Binns

"Familiar" portrait images:
Titian – man in padded blue jacket
Vermeers (in Holl)

SMALL
FRAGMENT
of classical
use Cera
insert

FLOWER
flowery hat

Rose Isabero e
Rose m Beth
Rose / Ca
Smelling a rose
giving a flower

Eve and Adam – working studies 2000 (left)

Audrey Walker in her studio – March 2000 (above)

Life is just a bowl of cherries 1995

Parallel Lives: Audrey Walker, Embroiderer and Teacher

Months before Audrey Walker was due to take up her post as head of embroidery and textiles at Goldsmiths' College in 1975, Donald Bowen, Curator of the Commonwealth Institute Art Gallery, offered her a one-woman embroidery exhibition. Many would have jumped at the chance, but anticipating the responsibilities of the job looming on the horizon, she judiciously declined the offer.

Her commitment to full-time teaching took priority, and it was this activity that for many years formed the daily structure of her life, stitching fitting in during evenings, weekends and college vacations. Within this routine, only two major pieces a year were usually possible, large pieces often taking as long as six to nine months to complete. The life of an independent artist – a desirable professional ideal for many – was not a realistic option for her. Financial security from teaching was essential, but over and above this, was the tremendous satisfaction from teaching itself. Then, as now, she needed to balance the solitary, pleasurable activities of looking, recording, stitching and making with social interaction and responsibility; her idealism and highly communicative personality demanding that she 'make things happen' in other spheres, be it teaching, external examining, selecting for exhibitions, or, more recently, chairing the Crafts Advisory Panel for the Arts Council of Wales.

Audrey Walker's experience as a teacher, and of different kinds of educational institutions is immense. She began as an art teacher at Leeds Girls' High School in the early 50s, moving on to London secondary schools in South Hampstead and Parliament Hill (one of the first comprehensives), followed by Whitelands College of Education in 1966, where she was principal lecturer in painting, and finally to Goldsmiths' College in 1975. Her contribution and influence at Goldsmiths' are widely acclaimed. Here she began as head of embroidery and textiles as the course switched momentously to B.A. from the respected Dip.A.D. (Diploma in Art and Design), under the previous leadership of Constance Parker (née Howard). As she recalls, almost in disbelief, money was no object in those days and she immediately expanded the facilities and studio space, as well as the number of visiting staff and technicians. Furthermore, she initiated the amalgamation of the embroidery, print and weave areas which was a phenomenal undertaking in the 70s.

At Goldsmiths' Audrey Walker was instrumental in establishing self-motivated learning. With no project based work, students followed their own instincts and ideas, guided by tutors in one-to-one sessions. She writes, 'My whole approach to teaching was to put students first – to ask them to initiate lines of thought and then to work with them'.

In this progressive atmosphere, individuals were free to experiment with material, process and idea, 'moving across various areas and incorporating <u>any</u> appropriate material or method into the making'. She held the view that technique was secondary to concept, that it must always be relevant to concept and never 'shoddy': 'Relevance and eloquence are essential'. She helped to shape the embryonic careers of many successful textile artists, encouraging them to be brave, validating their explorations, allowing risky work to happen. An exchange during her interview for the Goldsmiths' position hints at her philosophy: 'And how far would you allow your students to go?'. To which she replied: 'Oh, to the edge of the precipice, and just as they're about to fall over, I'd throw out a lifeline'. Many ambitious and talented people benefited from her liberal, caring approach, and as graduates were able to embark on a broad range of professional careers.

Audrey Walker found teaching an enjoyable, two-way process and passionately believed in it. Teaching nurtured her as she nurtured her students. Of course there were obvious frustrations as a teacher, but ultimately she reaped the rewards of interacting with bright students; their stimulating textile and feminist debates prompting her to reflect upon and take new steps in her own practice. She writes, 'The teaching was an inevitable interruption ... on the other hand, the contact with students and staff would give me a boost (courage?) or maybe just <u>determination</u> to keep going – you can't sit back when all around are exploring, inventing, making'.

Let us now examine her own practice as an artist and embroiderer from the early years of her education to the present. It is a period of almost sixty years, a span that has witnessed seismic shifts in fine art practice and training in Britain, and many notable changes in the course of her work.

As a student of fine art for seven years, first at Edinburgh College of Art and then at the Slade, she was taught 'the crafts of drawing and painting, the ways in which you would represent something you perceived out there on a flat surface'. As practice at the Slade was entirely focused on the figure, she worked from the model five days a week every week. Having taken etching as a subsidiary subject, she reflects today on the connection between marks made in etching and those made in stitching. Not only was she learning her craft, she was also immersed in 'a moral thing, absolute honesty. You hadn't to fudge a mark, real Coldstream stuff, precision, precision; and if it wasn't quite right you had to scrape off a day's work'. Looking back now, she acknowledges how narrow and disciplined that training was, and questions why she never rebelled against it at the time. Reaction was to come years later at Goldsmiths'.

It was not until she became head of the art department at Parliament Hill in 1959, working with teachers responsible for pottery, textiles and sculpture, that she began to open her eyes to areas outside painting. Having more or less stopped painting herself, she stumbled across an exhibition of modern embroidery which was to change her life. From then on she began to regularly visit the British Museum to examine Coptic weaving and other textile artefacts she had never seriously considered before. Looking was followed by efforts at stitching, 'scribbling about' on a sewing machine at home usually reserved for dressmaking. Hooked, she spent two years learning stitching at evening classes run by the Embroiderers' Guild in Wimpole Street. Jan Beaney noticed her when she exhibited in one of the Guild's exhibitions and suggested she join the 62 Group. From 1966 to 1981 she was a regular participant in the organisation's exhibitions.

Almost everything she made from the 60s onwards is scattered to the four winds, purchased by public and private collectors all over the world. While she is certain of the destinies of many works – the Victoria and Albert Museum, the Embroiderers' Guild, school collections in Bedfordshire, Kent and Leicestershire, for example – numerous small embroideries remain untraced.

When we met to talk about early work, there were sadly no real objects to see and touch, only slide reproductions which nevertheless sparked off very valuable conversation.

Works from the 60s, such as *Mother and Child* (1962), were in tune with the dominant embroidery style of the period: flat, frontal, formalised to a certain extent and highly decorative. But then she began to look at the Cumberland landscape of her youth and a new direction suggested itself. In *First Snow* (1970), formal design was replaced by a

much freer kind of composition in which 'things went off the edge'. Similar concerns could be found in *Pool in the Garden* (1971), inspired by the Portuguese house and burnt out landscape where she spent her summers. As she recalls, both works were considered very avant-garde at the time. Over the next few years she evolved a distinct personal style, as typified by *Garden Patchwork* (1972) which referred to the traditional techniques of Irish patchwork and American quilts. For a brief spell, 'recovering [her] background', she investigated the rag rug tradition of northern England. This led to *Thunderstorm* (1976), a dense, weighty piece in which she subverted the prodding technique by working from one side first and then the other. It was a path she decided not to pursue.

A real breakthrough came with *Summer Window* (1977), a remarkable collage combining fragments of oil painting and net curtain, overstitched by machine and hand. She feels that

this piece represents 'what [she] wanted to be about' more than any other previous work. It was followed by a steady flow of embroideries which, coinciding with regular visits to Greece, were motivated by the landscape and her response to the qualities of Mediterranean light.

Significant examples in this group include the free-hanging quilts, *Summer Piece* (1977), *Golden Pieced Fabric* (1977–78) and *Golden Kastraki* (1986), all of which represent a break from her customary choice of a framed and mounted format. In *Summer Piece* she was ruthless about cutting and replacing sections, her handling of materials and interest in abstraction heralding a new freedom in British embroidery. Her stitching had become noticeably simpler as she built up layer upon layer of thread and cloth, 'eliminating all

First snow 1970 – detail (left)
Summer piece 1977 – detail (right)

Summer window 1977 – detail

decorative and formal stitches'. The pieced and patched *Golden Kastraki*, incorporating hand-stitching and bits of padding to catch the light, is, as she observes today, 'the nearest to abstract work [she has] ever done'.

These golden memories of sunlit, idyllic places, far away from grey London skies, were counterbalanced by an interest in feminism, prompted by conversations with students in the 70s about the intimate links between the development of the craft of embroidery and the development of women's status in society. She began to look more closely at her mother's textiles which she had rejected as a teenager, once exclaiming to her that '[she] would never waste [her] time poking with a needle'. Eventually she begged for her mother's tablecloths and began to work them into her own pieces, including the nostalgically entitled *Life is just a bowl of cherries* (1982), one of her best known embroideries. Here she 'recovered and celebrated the domestic dimension of women's lives, their concern with making the home beautiful', indeed everything she had vehemently rebelled against as a young woman. Autobiographical in nature, it may be seen

as a reconciliatory piece: two different hands in a single work symbolising the settlement of earlier differences between mother and daughter. On a less personal level, it explores the interplay between a real, flat, embroidered tablecloth and the stitched illusion of a three-dimensional bowl and solid fruit.

In the series *Thank you René* (1992–93), she returned to the still life in tribute to Magritte's painting *Ceci n'est pas une pipe* on the theme of the nature of illusion. In *This is not an apple* (1993), she reused pieces of her mother's intricately worked tray cloths, enjoying the juxtaposition between flat reality and her own illusion of fruit. A more ambitious still life followed, showing an aerial view of a large bowl of fruit on floating layers of real tablecloth, shadow and a stitched reproduction of a kelim rug. As she comments, 'When you work figuratively, the whole notion of representation becomes an issue'.

About this time she found herself drawn towards the figure in the landscape, producing *Walk to the Quiet Valley* (1991) and *These Golden Days* (1992). Both portray a lone figure in a golden-tinted, pastoral setting, each gazing away from the viewer and holding an orange; one appears to

'This is not an apple' 1993 – detail

'Life is just a bowl of cherries' 1982 – detail

Still-life 1993

Beach Woman 1996 – detail (right)

move along a path, absorbed in the moment, the other stands still, seemingly deep in contemplation. She has written of these works: 'I became aware that it was my own intrusion into that landscape which interested me. I was not so much concerned to give a faithful rendering of a particular place but rather to reflect the sensations of being absorbed into that space'.[1]

In 1996 she reached a major turning point in her embroidery career. Preoccupation with her own presence in the landscape shifted to observations of and speculation about casual seaside encounters between men and women, culminating in the arresting, larger than life heads and haunting mutual gazes of *Beach Man* and *Beach Woman*, their grand scale suggesting heroic status. From this point, the gaze, meetings and encounters became key themes, manifesting themselves in idealised heads amalgamated from memory and imagination. She speaks of her fascination with the power of the gaze in art across centuries: 'After five hundred years, a gaze in a Piero della Francesca painting can still make a profound connection'.

Towards the end of 1999, faces of people she actually knows compelled her to draw from life again. There are new portraits of fellow embroiderer and friend Rozanne Hawksley in a decorative scarf, of Walt, a sculptor, and a self-portrait 'wearing a crazy rainbow hat, half in shadow, with my glasses on'. While it is still too early to assess the role of this new series, she suggests that it 'complements and reinforces the memory/imagination work'.

Audrey Walker finds it curious that 'the wheel has come full circle', that in her seventies she is enthralled by the same subject that engaged her as a young painter, that of the human figure and portraiture. And yet she is not really surprised, believing that 'an artist can only have so many ideas within a lifetime', that there is a kind of inevitability in 'revisiting' subjects, and that 'reflecting back on something is one of the most important things an artist can do'.

That she is drawn towards the human figure and the human face in her art should come as no surprise at all, since she is highly motivated to connect with people, exchange ideas, and help others achieve their goals. Indeed her figurative subject-matter and her immeasurable contributions to education and public life serve as powerful testimonies to her love of humanity.

Amanda Fielding

Notes
[1] Audrey Walker, Observations, Memories and Encounters, Audrey Walker, Art of the Stitch with Insights, exhibition catalogue, 1999. All other quotations taken from Audrey Walker in conversation with or correspondence to Amanda Fielding, 1999–2000

Mrs Beasley – 1951
A final year oil painting at the Slade which won the
prize for 'Best Painting from the Head'. The model
took the same pose for twenty days – this was the
usual time taken for a portrait at the Slade.
Collection of the artist

Notes on the early work – Audrey Walker

Waterfall – early 1960's – detail (right)
I took many photographs in the Cumbrian fells and
then worked directly with applied areas of leather
and net, drawing into them with the slub yarns we
were all so excited with at the time.
Collection of the V&A Museum

First Snow – 1970 (below)
The Cumbrian landscape continued to inspire my
work. This small embroidery was typical of my work
at the time – freely cut areas of various fabrics
were combined with hand stitching.
Private collection UK

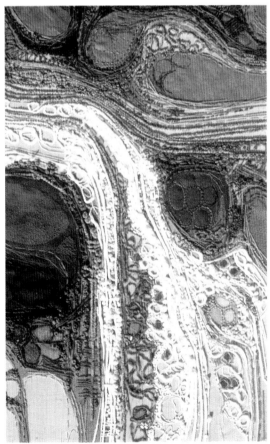

Monarchy 1000 – 1973 (below)
I do not enjoy working to commission but this
challenge was difficult to resist – a thousand years
of English monarchy to be told in one panel, for
permanent exhibition in Bath's Pump Room. The
same technique of cut, apply and stitch allowed
me to devise a free-flowing central area.
Collection of Bath City Council

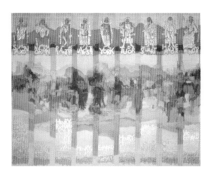

Summer Window – 1977 (above and right)
At last, in this piece, I arrived at ways of handling
my materials without restriction or preconception. I
relished every moment of its making and even
enjoyed seeing it again years later (in the
exhibition *Beyond the Dovetail* at the Crafts
Council). The motif of a net curtain makes a first
appearance here – re-appearing in much of my
current work. (122 x 152cm)
Collection of Sheila Paine

Golden Pieced Fabric – 1977/78
The brilliance of the light and the burnt out golden colours of Greece were now the basis of many years work. This free-hanging textile was constructed by cutting, piecing, re-cutting and overlaying until a coherent arrangement was achieved. (183 x 152cm)
Collection of Moira Gang

Golden Kastraki – 1986
I attempted to describe light and atmosphere in this 'almost abstract' textile. Torn strips of fabric were pieced together, over stitched and padded to give a shimmering layer of colour. Based upon drawings of a particular bay in Greece.
Collection of Mr & Mrs Reginald Hine

Summer Piece – 1977
A similar subject to *Golden Pieced Fabric*, this piece was made with many layers of machine stitching on pieced fabric. My inhibitions about the use of a sewing machine were now resolved. (76 x 61cm)
Collection of Susan Chivers

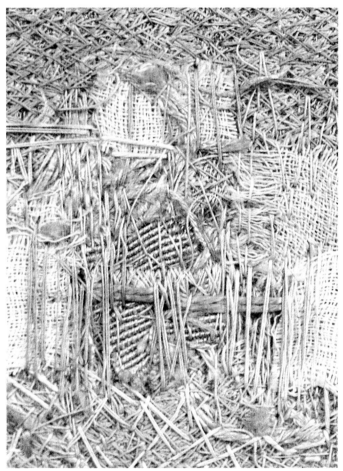

'Life is just a bowl of cherries' – 1982
So many ideas were brought together
in this piece and seemed to touch a
chord with other people that I was
prevailed upon to make several
versions. I celebrated my mother's
domestic embroidery (incorporating a
tablecloth circa 1935), used my love
of thirties popular songs and enjoyed
the puzzle of reality and illusion.
Private collection Italy

'Life is just a little bowl
of cherries' – 1984
Collection of Jan and Steve Udall

'Life is just a *(another)* bowl
of cherries' – 1995
*Collection of Bedfordshire
County Council*

'There's a rainbow round my shoulder' – 1983
As with the cherries, a thirties popular song
provided the idea, and again I incorporated one
of my mother's thirties tablecloths. (152 x 152cm)
Collection of Mr & Mrs W A Davies

Walk to the Quiet Valley – 1991
After years of working primarily with a landscape
theme this was an important move to re-introduce
the human figure, partly prompted by thoughts
about 'representation' (as in the still life pieces) it
was mainly about my own existence in a particular
space and about a 'moment' – a figure in a
landscape integrating the two aspects – almost a
self-portrait?
Private collection (USA)

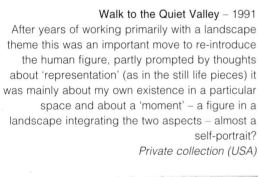

Walk in Asini – 1992
On a similar theme to the
Quiet Valley, but on a
smaller scale and largely
machine stitched.
Collection of Michael Green

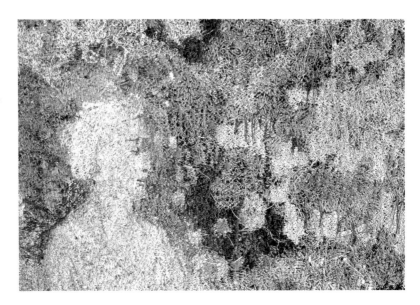

'This is not an apple' – 1993
The impact of a superb Magritte exhibition and the loss of my
workroom (before rebuilding in Wales) led to a series of small
embroideries – the *Thank you René* series. Reality and illusion
(using a 'real' table-mat flat but stitching an illusion of reality)
and a playful enjoyment of these were my main thoughts.
Collection of Moira Vincentelli

Still-life – 1993 – details
With a new workroom I could embark on larger
pieces and it seemed logical to summarise all
the little still-life motifs – and to include a small
tribute to Morandi – a master of still-life.
Collection of Jan and Steve Udall

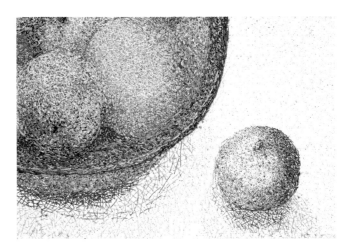

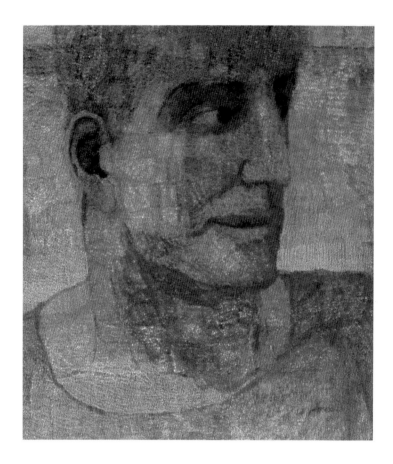

Beach Man – 1995
Larger than life size and therefore suggestive of
'heroes', these two works focused my thoughts
about encounters, momentary glances,
vulnerability, and the power of a gaze. They have
led me towards all my work since 1995.
Collection of Pat Starr

Beach Woman – 1996
Collection of the artist

A Cumbrian Birthday – 1997/8

Approaching my seventieth birthday I decided to celebrate my West Cumbrian childhood. Although this is a private family piece, anyone with Cumbrian connections will recognise the traditional rum-butter bowl and may recall a little ritual around the birth of a baby. Hand embroidery on my mother's cloth.
Collection of the artist

Legend behind A Cumbrian Birthday

There was a Cumbrian tradition which my parents followed when I was born – When relatives and friends came to see a new baby they would be offered a glass of port and cream crackers with rum-butter. This was set out on the bedside table, on an embroidered cloth, with the special rum-butter bowl, the best glasses and plates which usually came from the wedding china. The bowl, plate and glass shown in this embroidery were certainly beside my mother's bed. The cloth is one of many which were used on tables or trays in our home.

3rd July 1928

Andrew 2000

Curriculum Vitae

Education
1944–48   Edinburgh College of Art, Diploma in Art
1948–51   Slade School of Fine Art, Diploma in Fine Art

Awards
1993   MBE for Services to Art, especially Embroidery

Work in Public Collections (selected)
V&A Museum, National Gallery of New South Wales, the Department of the Environment, the Embroiderers' Guild, the Pump Room in Bath, Bedfordshire, Kent, Leicestershire and Reading Schools collections.

Work in Private Collections in
Australia, Canada, Eire, Italy, USA and UK

Group Exhibitions (selected)
1966–81   62 GROUP exhibitions: UK and overseas at venues including V&A Museum, National Museum of Wales, Commonwealth Institute, Bradford Museum, TUC Headquarters, Greenwich Theatre Gallery
1966   Embroiderers' Guild Diamond Jubilee, Commonwealth Institute
1966   Ecclesiastical Embroidery, St Paul's Cathedral Crypt, London
1969   Ecclesiastical Embroidery, Chapter House, York
              Pictures For Schools, London
1970   Pictures For Schools, National Museum of Wales
1972   Embroiderers' Guild International Members, Commonwealth Institute
1976   Opening Exhibition – Textural Art Gallery, London
              Embroiderers' Guild Members – Commonwealth Institute
1977   Textiles by Artist Craftsmen – Southampton Gallery
1982   Stitchery, British Craft Centre
              17 Super Stitchers, Oxford Gallery
1983   Textiles Staff, Goldsmiths College Gallery
              Embroidery, Doddington Hall, Lincolnshire
1986   Threads International, Aldeburgh, Suffolk
1991   Resident Artists, Haystack, Maine, USA
              Beyond the Dovetail, Crafts Council
1992   Out Of The Frame, Crafts Council
1993   Selectors, National Eisteddfod, Builth Wells

1994   Stitched Impressions, Forge Mill Needle Museum
1996–98 ARTextiles, Bury St Edmunds and touring
1997   Wales Drawing Biennale, Aberystwyth and touring
1998   50 x 50, 62 GROUP, Israel, London and Dublin
           Cloths of Gold, Contemporary Applied Arts, London
           9 Artists, Oriel Myrddin, Carmarthen
1999   Cloths of Gold at Threads of Life, Yarlington, Somerset
           Insights (3 person), Barbican Centre, London, and Shipley Art Gallery, Gateshead
2000   Solo touring exhibition – The Gallery, Ruthin Craft Centre

Journals and Publications (selected)

'Needlework, an Illustrated History' – Bridgeman and Dury – Paddington Press 1978
'World of Embroidery' – profile – Summer Issue 1983 – Vol. 34. No 2.
'Twentieth Century Embroidery in Great Britain' – Constance Howard – BT Batsford 1986
'Stitches & Embroidery – New Approaches' – Jan Beaney – BT Batsford 1985
'The Art Of The Needle' – Jan Beaney – Century/Hutchingson (Australia) 1988
'A Complete Guide to Creative Embroidery' – Jan Beaney – BT Batsford 1991
'British Craft Textiles' – Ann Sutton – Collins 1995
'Sources of Inspiration' by Pamela Johnson – Crafts magazine, No. 145, March/April 1997
'World of Embroidery' – profile 'Powerful observations' by Maggie Grey – March 1999 – Vol. 50. No. 2.
'Art of The Stitch with Insights' – exhibition catalogue, 1999 Embroiderers' Guild ISBN 0 903562 30 8
'Fiberarts' – Nov/Dec 1999 – Vol. 26. No. 3.

Teaching

1951–54 Leeds Girls High School, Art Teacher
1954–57 South Hampstead High School, Art Teacher
1959–66 Parliament Hill Comprehensive School, Head of Art Dept
1966–75 Whitelands College, Principal Lecturer in Painting
1975–88 Goldsmiths College, Head of Dept of Embroidery/Textiles
1975–94 Visiting lecturer at colleges, polytechnics and universities throughout the UK, including:
           University of Ulster, University of London Institute of Education, Royal College of Art,
           Glasgow School of Art, Exeter College of Art; In the USA – Boston University,
           Washington University (St Louis), Cranbrook Academy (Detroit)
1973–   Speaker/Teacher at Conferences and Textiles Summer Schools including Aberystwyth
           Arts Centre, Barry Summer School (South Glamorgan), Embroiderers' Guild (UK and
           Australia), V&A Museum
1991   Haystack Mountain School of Crafts (Maine, USA), Resident Artist

Examining

1973–76 London University and Bristol University Institutes of Education, B.Ed.Art
1976–78 Trent Polytechnic, BA Hons Textiles
1981–85 Birmingham Polytechnic, MA Textiles
1981–85 Middlesex Polytechnic, BA Hons Textiles
1983   Jacob Kramer College, Leeds, Foundation Level
1984   Falmouth School of Art, Foundation Level
1985–88 Sunderland Polytechnic, BA Art, Design and Craft
1986–89 University of Ulster, Belfast, BA Hons Textiles/Embroidery
1988–91 Edinburgh College of Art, BA Hons Tapestry
1989–91 Windsor and Maidenhead FE College, City and Guilds Advanced Diploma

Other Professional Activities

1979–86 Member CNAA Fashion/Textiles Board (Vice Chair 1984–86)
1980–82 Member, Crafts Council Textiles Panel
1980–82 Member, Crafts Council Education Panel
1980   Advisor, 4th International Miniature Textiles Exhibition
1981   Selector, 'Textiles North' Exhibition

1983–84   Member, Crafts Council 'Texstyles' Projects Panel
1984–85   Selector, British Council, British Artists for LODZ Triennale Tapestry Exhibition
1984–86   Chairman, Association of Heads of Textiles & Fashion Degree Courses
1985–86   Selector, Embroiderers' Guild/RIBA Exhibition of Stitched Textiles
1985–87   Governor, Loughborough College of Art and Design
1990   Selector, Embroiderers' Guild, Exhibition of Stitched Textiles at the Commonwealth
           Institute
1991   Selector/Curator, Embroiderers' Guild, 'In Context'
1992   Selector, Crafts Council, 'Out Of The Frame' Exhibition
1993   Selector, Art and Craft, National Eisteddfod of Wales
1993–97   Chair, Fishguard Arts Society
           Co–ordinator, Last Invasion Tapestry Project, Fishguard
1994–98   Member, Arts Council of Wales, Crafts Board
1998–99   Chair, Arts Council of Wales, Crafts Advisory Panel
1998–99   Member, Arts Council of Wales Artform Development Committee
1998–   Chair, Fishguard Invasion Centre Trust Ltd

Profile, Kate 1997

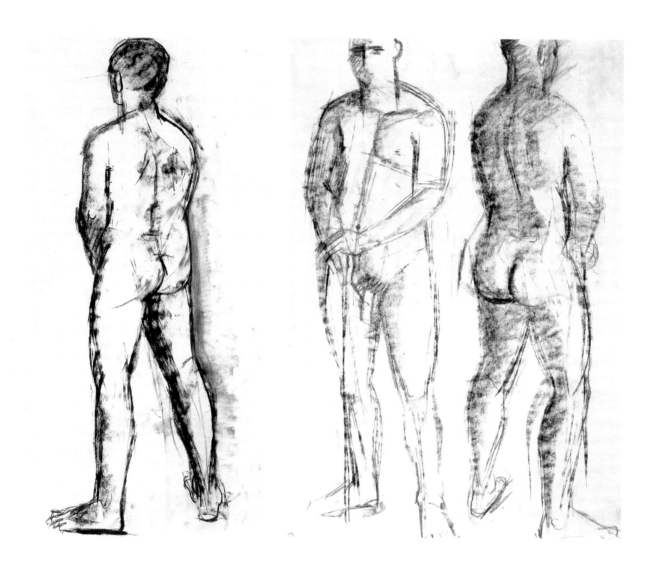

Andrew standing, back view 2000

Andrew, back and front 2000

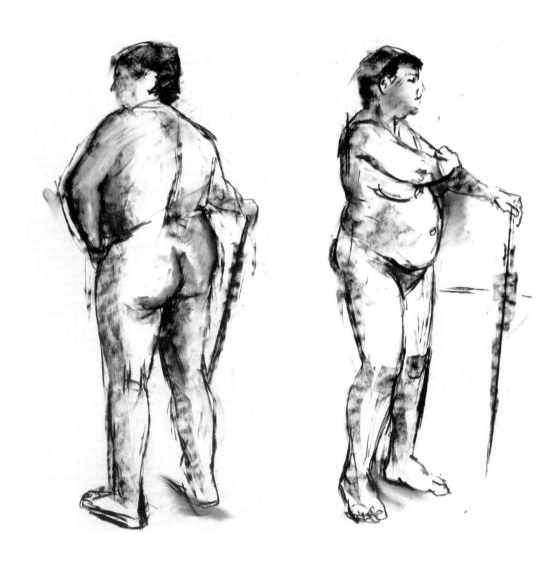

Gina, back view 2000

Gina and parasol 2000

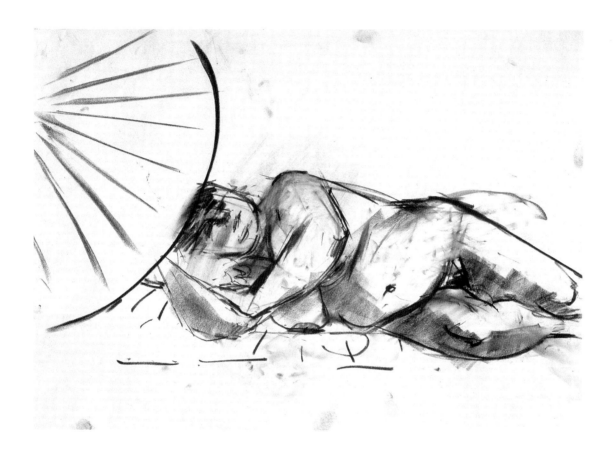

Under a parasol 1999

Gina in a sunhat 1999

Afterwords......

Audrey Walker has been an important influence to many textile artists throughout the UK – below five textile art practitioners comment.

Michael Brennand-Wood

'Few people in life exert an influence so profound that it would be hard to imagine life without them. Audrey Walker's influence, guidance and friendship has certainly changed my life.

An invitation to visit the textile dept at Goldsmiths' in 1977 led to my first teaching position. Most importantly Audrey gave me the opportunity to engage at first hand in the most fundamental exciting change in the development of new textile expression. Audrey's vision encouraged a pluralist approach to subject matter, her pioneering emphasis on ideas as opposed to technique changed irrevocably the way textiles would be taught in colleges and schools in the future.

Audrey's own studio work is equally characterised by a sustained commitment to the developmental. Effortlessly skillful, her most recent figuratives pieces are I believe some of the most exciting textiles I've ever seen. Audrey's work represents a unique synthesis of colour, thread and image, a consummate fusion of stitched and painterly sources.

Spectacularly modest for one who has influenced so many, if there is one defining quality that unifies all aspects of Audrey's life then it would be Integrity.'

Michael Brennand-Wood – is internationally known as an artist, curator, lecturer and arts consultant, his work is in major public and corporate collections worldwide, including the V&A, Whitworth, and Crafts Council collections – a book *'Michael Brennand-Wood – You Are Here'* was published in 1999 by the Hare Press ISBN 0 9535847 1 2.

Rozanne Hawksley

'One of the exhibits in the joyful Festival of Britain in 1951, was an automated arm waving a kind of benediction. It was gloved in purple velvet and labelled, if I remember correctly, '...the iron hand in the velvet glove' – a deceptive combination of strength and flexibility. In the way I use it here it could also read '...the velvet hand in the iron glove' – both versions of the epigram being appropriate to and descriptive of Audrey Walker, artist, craftsman, teacher, head of department and now friend. Others have written and will write eloquently of her and of her contribution to Art – in particular Textile Art. Her work speaks for itself and the integrity plus commitment shines out. To have been one of her students and subsequently a member of her staff is to have been given unforeseeable, far reaching rewards. Rewards that are perpetual and infinite. Thank you Audrey.'

Rozanne Hawksley – lives near Audrey in West Wales, she studied at Goldsmiths as a mature student after training at Royal College of Art and following a successful career in fashion and lecturing, she has work in several collections including the Imperial War Museum and recently completed a major commission for the Bishop of London's mitre.

Alice Kettle

'Audrey has always recognised the huge potential of textile art as something that is challenging, provocative and expansive. Her vision is especially about people. Audrey could see in me what I didn't realise myself, and I know that I am not alone. I was enabled to see my vision of the future by her. Nothing was forced upon me but my eyes were opened, my life was changed! I anticipate this new exhibition with great excitement.'

Alice Kettle – studied at Goldsmiths, has exhibited widely and completed a number of notable major public commissions, her work is included in several collections including those of the Whitworth and the Crafts Council, a monograph *'The eye of the Needle – the Textile art of Alice Kettle'* was published in 1996 by Telos.

Shelly Goldsmith

'A pioneer in making textile works that go beyond the pictorial to investigate the expressive use of materials, line and mood. From early on, and at a distance (for we have never met), Audrey Walker opened my eyes to the potential of the medium of textiles. Her work, both professionally and in education makes bold statements, blurs boundaries and has engendered an experimental and challenging environment for the textile artist. Ultimately making a profound impact on contemporary textile practice.'

Shelly Goldsmith – works at the forefront of contemporary tapestry, she has been featured in exhibitions worldwide and was recently in 'Ripe' the first exhibition in the Crafts Council's 3Up series profiling work by rising stars in the applied arts (catalogue ISBN 1870145 95 X) – a graduate of the Tapestry MA at Royal College of Art with work in several public collections, she is Programme Leader in BA Textile Art at Winchester School of Art.

Eleri Mills

'Audrey Walker was someone I long admired at a distance. From the late seventies onwards, her work always shone out for me in any group exhibition, and seemed quite distinctive in its nature and level of sophistication – the method of work used was so painterly and expressive – the subject matter would always be thoughtful, sometimes passionate and profound – all Audrey Walker's work demonstrates her ability to draw. More recently since her move to Wales, she has taken on a new role for me – a kind of honorary 'Aunt' whose influence I value very much.'

Eleri Mills – was winner of Art of the Stitch prize in 1999 and profiled in the USA's 'Fiberarts' magazine, her 1995 solo exhibition premiered at the Museu Tèxtil d'Indumentària in Barcelona before touring the UK during 1996–7, (catalogue 'Eleri Mills' published by RCC 1995, ISBN 1 85991 022 X) pieces have been purchased by the Whitworth and the National Library of Wales collections.

Secret smiles – working studies 1998

List of plates

Early work

Rozanne 1999 (above)

Walt 1997 (left)

Liz 2000 (opposite)

h x w (all in cms)

Published by The Gallery, Ruthin Craft Centre
Text © the authors and RCC 2000
ISBN 1 900941 28 7
Printed by Midas Colour

acknowledgements
Ruthin Craft Centre would like to thank and acknowledge the
assistance of the following: Jennifer Harris; the Arts Council of
Wales Visual Art and Craft Department; John Hambley; Sandra
Bosanquet; Roger Lefevre; Jill Piercy; Eleri Mills; Polly Binns;
Amanda Fielding; Lisa Daniel at the Crafts Council Shop; Doreen
Daniel; Christine Mills; Rozanne Hawksley; Alice Kettle; Michael
Brennand-Wood; Shelly Goldsmith; Nicola Heywood-Thomas, Erica
Hossington and staff at HTV's High Performance; Moira Vincentelli;
Mary Schoeser; Dewi Tannatt Lloyd; Shawn Stipling; Dave Lewis;
Hafina Clwyd; Fennah Podschies; Seán Harris; Pete Goodridge.

Audrey Walker would like to thank and acknowledge the assistance
of:-'all those who have helped and supported me during the
development of this exhibition, and throughout a long career;
particular thanks to friends Rozanne Hawksley and Eirian Short for
healthy criticism and positive support during the inevitable 'down'
patches; John at Robel Framers Haverfordwest and Richard at
Sessions Gallery Newport; to Dewi Tannatt Lloyd for patient,
meticulous and sensitive photography of my work; and to my ex-
students – their successes are an ongoing joy and inspiration.'

Designed by Aquarium 01244 398004

Photography – by Dewi Tannatt Lloyd (historical photography – pre
1995 works except Mrs Beasley – by Audrey Walker)

Ruthin Craft Centre Exhibition staff:
Philip Hughes & Jane Gerrard

'Audrey Walker' is a Ruthin Craft Centre Touring Exhibition with
support from the Arts Council of Wales.

*This exhibition catalogue is also available in a Welsh Language
Version.*

The Gallery
Ruthin Craft Centre,
Park Road, Ruthin, Denbighshire,
North Wales LL15 1BB
Tel: 01824 704774

Ruthin Craft Centre is part of Denbighshire County Council.